*Quick*GUIDES
everything you need to know...fast

ACQUIRING NEW DONORS

by Graham McKern

reviewed by Michelle Campbell

WIREMILL
PUBLISHING LTD

Across the world the organizations and institutions that fundraise to finance their work are referred to in many different ways. They are charities, non-profits or not-for-profit organizations, non-governmental organizations (NGOs), voluntary organizations, academic institutions, agencies, etc. For ease of reading, we have used the term Nonprofit Organization, Organization or NPO as an umbrella term throughout the *Quick*Guide series. We have also used the spellings and punctuation used by the author.

Published by
Wiremill Publishing Ltd.
Edenbridge, Kent TN8 5PS, UK
info@wiremillpublishing.com
www.wiremillpublishing.com
www.quickguidesonline.com

British Library Cataloguing in Publication Data
A catalogue record for this book is available from the British Library.

ISBN Number 1-905053-24-X

Printed by Rhythm Consolidated Berhad, Malaysia
Cover Design by Jennie de Lima and Edward Way
Design by Colin Woodman Design

Disclaimer of Liability
The author, reviewer and publisher shall have neither liability nor responsibility to any person or entity with respect to any loss or damage caused or alleged to be caused directly or indirectly by the information contained in this book. While the book is as accurate as possible, there may be errors, omissions or inaccuracies.

Contents

INTRODUCTION

Your organization relies on donors for long-term sustainability. If it doesn't need donors, then this book is not for you!

Donors bring vitally needed resources to help fulfill your organization's purpose. A donation by a donor should be regarded as active approval and encouragement for your mission.

Because donors cannot live forever and their income streams vary during different life stages, loss of donors will inevitably occur. For example, imagine you had 100 people giving donations two years ago. It is highly unlikely that all of these people will still be giving today. Some may have moved without notifying you, while others may have decided to give to another cause instead. This loss of donors is called natural attrition.

Acquiring new donors to offset this natural attrition is not only a sensible way to maintain, and potentially grow, your donation stream, but is also a vital requirement to sustain your organization.

This book specifically focuses on acquiring donors of funds. However, much of the advice given can equally apply to acquiring new members or new volunteers who will give gifts of time and ability.

This Guide explores who to target as well as why, where and how, and also compares different methods that you might use. It discusses the strategies needed to build on your success, how to start and how to evaluate your results.

WHY GROW OR BUILD A SUPPORTER BASE?

The key purpose of donors is to create resources to fulfill your organization's mission. Regular, long-term donors bring you a predictable source of funds. If you ask for their support and you have a case for why you need support, you generally can rely upon them to provide the resources you need.

Having a large pool of donors rather than just a few donors of large amounts provides several advantages to an organization:

- The more donors you have, the more funds that may be raised.

- A large number of donors insulates against the effects of donors who stop giving or reduce their support.

- The larger the pool of loyal donors, the more opportunity you have to cultivate major gifts and bequests.

- Having a significant pool of donors provides funds that can be used for a variety of purposes rather than just the specific purposes often imposed by large donors, particularly trusts and foundations. Individuals and smaller donors are often happy to have their funds used for general purposes such as operating expenses, while large donors often do not allow this flexibility.

EVALUATING BENEFITS OF A CAMPAIGN

You need to be clear about the reason why you are having a donor-acquisition campaign. Is it to find donors to raise immediate funds or is it an investment in the future? Often the costs of acquiring a new donor can equal or exceed the donations received and may not be the best way to fund immediate needs. But it is a way of ensuring the future of your organization. The actual financial benefit to your organization of a donor-acquisition campaign can be calculated.

1. Work out what the expected costs of the campaign will be.

2. Then estimate the number of responses you expect to receive. Your local direct marketing industry association should be able to advise you on the average response rate received by other organizations based upon the methods they used. Use this average percentage to calculate the actual number of donations you might expect to receive based upon the number of people you ask to give. For example, if the average response rate is 2 percent and you plan to contact 1,000 people, you can expect 20 responses.

3. Next, estimate the average donation size you expect to receive. Your organization may have run similar campaigns in the past. You can use figures from past campaigns as a guide. If not, you will need to make an educated guess based on the amounts you are seeking from the potential donors.

4. Multiply the average donation size expected by the number of donations you expect to receive, and you now have an estimate of the income that the campaign will bring in.

5. Finally, subtract the expenses of the campaign from the amount you anticipate receiving.

You may be surprised to find that the expenses will exceed the income, often by a significant amount. This exercise will help you clarify whether this donor-acquisition campaign is being undertaken to generate immediate funds or to create a pool of loyal, long-term donors.

After you have looked at the possible initial returns from the donor-acquisition campaign, you can then look at the long-term benefits of the campaign.

If you have current donor records, they can be analyzed to calculate what your average donor gives annually. If not, based upon the average donation size you expect to receive, conservatively estimate what the annual income might be from your new donors.

How many of your new donors do you think will give a second and subsequent time? Is it 60 percent or 50 percent or even 30 percent? Again, if you have current donor records, you should be able to accurately calculate what percentage of donors will give more than once. If you don't have current records, you can ask other, similar organizations for their experiences. Many organizations find that between 50 percent and 60 percent of donors give a second and subsequent time.

1. Work out how many donors will give more than once and multiply this number of donors by the average annual donation you expect to receive from them in the next year.

2. Then work out how much this might be in the second year, and the third, making allowance for some natural attrition. A reasonable percentage of natural attrition is 15 percent a year.

You can now calculate the future income you might expect from these new donors. If your campaign is expected to break even within a year or so, it would be a very wise investment. If it isn't expected to break even, don't proceed with the campaign or determine if a different style of campaign is appropriate, one that costs less or increases the number of respondents or the value of their donations.

REVIEWER'S COMMENT
Be prepared for the fact that donor acquisition is very costly. That is why it needs to be done right. The cost of donor acquisition can sometimes be equal to the campaign income. Clearly the purpose is to find new donors, not to raise money in the first instant. The goals and the related costs of donor acquisition need to be clearly understood within an organization so that everyone involved understands the objectives as they relate to monetary return on investment.

If you already have donors, start by thinking about them.

- Where do they live? Are there geographical areas where most of your donors live? Why is this? Does your cause have high visibility or presence in that area? If not, why has this area yielded a high number of donors in the past? Are there likely to be more donors in this area who can be identified?

- Why are your donors supporting you now? Do they support your organization specifically or do they support your cause? For example, some people want to find a solution for homelessness and will fund any organization working in that area that asks for their support. Others might want to give to a specific organization because of its reputation for the quality of its work in helping homeless people. If you don't know why people give to your organization, ask current donors. You can do this by telephone, by meeting with them and asking them, or by a mail survey. Having a conversation with your donor is usually much better than a mail survey because you can also use this opportunity to build your relationship with him or her. Ultimately you are trying to discover if there are common reasons that donors support your organization. Are there likely to be more donors who would support you for those same reasons?

- Is there a common belief system or experience among your donors? Are they linked by religious affiliation, school attendance, love of animals, interest in the same illness, etc.? Are there more people in the community who share these beliefs or interests?

- What is it about your cause that is compelling enough for your donors to give to you? Again, ask them if you don't know. Are there others in the community who would give if they knew about these compelling facts? How can you tell them?

- Where will you find people like your donors? Think about what you have discovered about your donors. What is the best way to reach them?

PROFILES OF POTENTIAL DONORS

If you don't have donors but want to acquire them for the first time, think about the previous questions to guide your thinking.

Test your answers. Speak with some people whose opinions you respect. Ask them questions about your organization, its standing in the community, and its reputation within the areas it works and among similar organizations. Write down what they say. You may need to speak with between five and ten people, but from these conversations you should get a fairly strong sense of common opinion.

Based upon this testing process, use this knowledge to build a broad profile of who a potential donor might be. Identifying likely donors to your organization is called donor profiling, and good donor profiling is crucial to the success of any campaign.

REVIEWER'S COMMENT
It is important to "qualify" a prospective donor to determine if his or her interest is a match with your organization. It is important that some qualifying or reasonable validation process be done before investing in donor acquisition or else your investment is a waste. Too many organizations fail to take this step, and they throw good money after bad as a result. They can end up abandoning donor-acquisition efforts in frustration, when a more strategic, careful approach would have yielded the right result.

MOTIVATING PEOPLE TO SUPPORT YOUR CAUSE

Once you've identified people who might be interested in supporting your cause, you then need to motivate them to do so. Knowledge about your organization – your brand recognition or lack of it – needs to be taken into account in designing an acquisition program. If people don't know who you are, they need to be educated about you before they will be interested in supporting you.

Trust and integrity are key ingredients in deciding to give to a cause. However, trust and integrity are not enough. In order for donors to open their hearts enough to give, your cause has to be compelling. Your organization also has to be seen as relevant and competent in its work. These five things – trust, integrity, compelling cause, relevance and competence – work together to encourage donors to be favorably disposed toward making a donation. They need to be the cornerstone of your acquisition campaign material.

The decision to give arises when donors have their needs met. This means concentrating on the donor and his or her needs rather than just the needs of your organization. There are a number of latent emotions within each of us. Use storytelling to highlight the work that your organization is doing. This gives an outlet for these emotions and persuades potential donors that they should act.

When creating leaflets, letters or advertisements, design your copy (the words used) to incorporate the following elements.

- Provide an outlet for emotions. Anger, fear, pity, love, concern, moral outrage, etc., are important emotions. They help us identify how we feel about an issue being described. They are also key motivators for giving.

- Access deeply held beliefs. It is true that most people have definite opinions about certain aspects of life. These can be based on political viewpoints, religious upbringing or faith experiences. People often hold philosophical or ideological views. If you have a clear view of your target audience, you can use appropriate copy and graphics to align your organization with these beliefs.

- Bring out a sense of duty or obligation.

- Encourage loyalty. Research findings across the world indicate that people value loyalty. How can you use this fact in your copy and graphics? Words such as "friends," "neighbors" and "community" all build upon this sense of loyalty.

- Involve the donor. Donors like to feel that their donations make a real difference. You need to ensure that your copy and graphics involve the donors. Make donors feel that by supporting you, they are helping solve a problem. Loyalty to your organization is what you set out to achieve in donor acquisition!

- Offer the chance for prestige. Most donors like to be made to feel special, whether they admit it or not. Think about offers you can make in your copy. Can you create donor-recognition opportunities? For example, can you offer the opportunity for the first 50 new donors to your cause to attend a cocktail party with a local celebrity?

- Provide access to important people. Providing access to important people can be a strong motivation for giving. For example, an environmental organization could sponsor an intimate forum with political leaders charged with the responsibility of caring for the environment. The forum could be open to all those who give above a designated amount of money.

It is important to remember that the donor-acquisition program must work as part of the overall strategy of your organization in marketing itself, in its donor-retention programs, with its special events, and with the work it undertakes. The items that have been mentioned here should be seen in the context of what is appropriate for your organization and its larger strategy.

REVIEWER'S COMMENT

Caution needs to be exercised when talking about emotion. It's the goal of fund-development storytelling to "pull at the heart strings," but an organization also risks going too far and being perceived as "exploiting" those cared for by the organization. There is also the risk of embellishment or overstatement of case. This kind of emotive storytelling is a true communication skill that needs to be honed appropriately and can take a fund-development professional years to develop.

There are a number of methods you can use during your campaign. They range vastly in time, trouble, expense, and response. Keep in mind that the goal of acquisition is to gain donors who will give and keep giving, not give once and then move on to another organization.

Your governing body needs to be prepared to invest funds and produce an effective campaign rather than seek cheap solutions. Remember, the long-term sustainability of your organization is at stake.

Contact your local direct marketing industry association to find out who can provide you with lists of people who fit your donor profile and to whom you can send direct mail. You might also recruit volunteers from the private sector with experience in direct mail strategy to advise you. There is a great deal to be learnt from these experts.

Suppliers often have lists compiled from shopper surveys, from specific product purchases, from voter registration records, or built around lifestyle characteristics, to name just a few. These lists are usually available for rent. The suppliers will provide the names and addresses of people, who fit your chosen profile, for a fee. You can use a list only once; if people respond to you, you can retain information about them. Lists are usually seeded with dummy names so that the supplier can ensure that you use the list just once. Sometimes it is possible to purchase a list whose names you can use more than once, but this needs to be clear at the time of purchase.

On the other hand, you may prefer to use the "mass" approach such as radio, television or newspapers to advertise your cause and seek a response. If this is your choice, then you need to research the audience demographics of these media outlets. You need to ensure that your approach reaches your target audience.

Another method of reaching potential donors is through leaflets mailed, distributed or handed out.

CAMPAIGN METHODS

You might consider distributing leaflets to a whole geographical area. This approach means that many people who receive your leaflet will not fit your target audience. So leaflet distribution needs to be carefully planned. For example, if you want to reach 18- to 25-year-old females, you might plan your leaflet drop at a university campus rather than in suburban mailboxes.

Another method, which is highly labour-intensive, is to personally give leaflets to people in the street who appear to fit your profile.

Contacting potential donors by telephone is a relatively new technique that offers significant benefits if done correctly, and even newer is contacting potential donors by email and through their mobile/cell phones.

Following is a discussion of the advantages and disadvantages of using the various methods to reach the donors whose profiles you have identified.

In all events ensure you comply with all laws and regulations relative to that method.

LEAFLETS
Leaflets are simple and economical to produce but must always contain a response mechanism, be it a tear-off slip, a telephone number to ring, or perhaps a website address to visit for more information. However, before using leaflets for your donor-acquisition campaign, consider their advantages and disadvantages.

Advantages
- They are easily produced, with many local printers able to produce them at very little cost.

Continues on next page

They can be relatively inexpensive to deliver to a large number of households. Methods can include insertion into a newspaper, delivery with other advertising to mailboxes, or by handing out to people in the street.

Some targeting can be achieved if you plan carefully. For example, you may decide to give them to people in the street who appear to be middle-aged or older, if that is your target market, or deliver them to places where your target market is likely to frequent.

Because the receivers of the leaflets have to initiate the response by contacting you, they will have an interest in your cause and potentially be more likely to become long-term supporters of your organization.

Disadvantages

Leaflets cannot be personalized for broad distribution. Therefore, your copy has limited ability to address all the motivational triggers previously described.

Because you have to write in generalities, unless your organization has a very high profile or your cause is seen as very urgent (such as a natural disaster), your response rate from leaflets is likely to be very small. It could be as little as two to five responses per thousand pieces delivered.

If the response rate is small, then the seemingly inexpensive production and distribution costs could actually be poor value for the money.

Mass media

Mass media such as newspapers, radio and television reach a significant number of people. You can place advertisements, send out press releases, or ask for an article to be written about or by your organization. All media outlets use the term "reach" to describe the number of people who could see or hear your message.

When evaluating different media, it is important that you understand the difference between potential reach and actual reach. For example, a local newspaper might have a potential reach (also known as distribution) of 50,000 people. This means that the newspaper is actually delivered into the hands of 50,000 people. Maybe only 30,000 people actually read the newspaper, and only 10,000 people actually read your advertisement or article. This is the "actual reach."

CAMPAIGN METHODS

Advantages

- Mass media have the potential to address a large number of people at one time.

- Press releases sent to media outlets may be printed or broadcast at no cost to your organization.

- The cost of getting your message out may appear to be expensive in actual cost but may be relatively inexpensive based on the potential reach. For example, if you divide the total cost by the potential reach, the cost may be very small.

- You will get a fairly instantaneous response, so you will know whether your message is getting through. If you are not getting a positive response, you can try something different.

- Again, because potential supporters have to initiate the response by contacting you, they are demonstrating their interest in your organization, making it much more likely that they will become donors.

- You can focus on a particular segment of the population by placing your advertising or press releases only with media outlets that appeal to your target audience.

Disadvantages

- Press releases are often altered or shortened, changing their impact. There is also the risk that they will not be printed or broadcast at all. The only sure way to get your message into the media is to pay for it as advertising.

- You need to check demographic data very carefully to ensure that the actual reach is good value for money.

- If you are using radio or television, you will need to repeat your advertising a number of times to ensure it is heard. Most marketing research suggests you will need to repeat your advertisement at least seven to ten times within one week to gain maximum actual reach. (Electronic media describe this as "frequency.")

- Your organization is competing with many other advertisers, and you have literally only a few seconds to grab attention. Be wary of purely attention-grabbing advertising. Sometimes this will not sit comfortably with your organization's mission and values.

- Again, unless your organization has a very high profile or your cause

Continues on next page

has a strong sense of urgency, your response rate is likely to be very small. In addition, it will not be easy to measure what worked and what didn't if you are using more than one media outlet.

PERSONALIZED MAIL

Personalized mail requires you to know your target audience. You will need to obtain lists of names and addresses, and your letter will need to address the motivational triggers that are associated with people who fit your profile.

Advantages

- Mail is highly targeted. It should be addressed only to those people who fit your target profile.

- It can be tailored to your budget. You can mail to as many or to as few people as your budget allows.

- Your message can be delivered on the same day to everyone on your target list.

- Your message can be the same to every prospect with no variation other than mail personalization.

- Or you can vary the message, as well as how the mail is sent, how people are invited to respond, and other factors to see what works best. (Be careful that you only change one variable when testing. Otherwise, your test results will be useless.)

- A result will be known relatively quickly, often within days, and most likely will continue for several weeks. It is not uncommon to receive an occasional response several months later.

- The response rate for personalized mail is generally much higher than for leaflets or mass media. Anecdotally, the response seems to be about five times greater.

Disadvantages

- You don't know what happens to your mail when it is received. Perhaps your mail is thrown away without being opened. Perhaps it is read and then thrown in the bin. You also don't know what emotions are evoked, if any, in the prospect. The only response you know about is the positive response when a donation arrives.

- You don't know if the names of prospects and their mailing addresses are correct. You only know they are incorrect when mail is returned.

■ Mail preparation and postage are often more expensive than leaflet distribution or mass media. This disadvantage is overcome if the response rate is sufficient to justify the cost.

TELEPHONE

Donor acquisition by telephone is becoming very popular. Known as telemarketing, it has significant advantages and disadvantages that need to be considered.

Advantages

■ Telemarketing gives an instantaneous response. If prospects hate your message, they'll tell you.

■ If the response is not up to your expectations, you can change the script used by those making calls on your behalf.

■ If what you are asking the prospects to do is not realistic, they will let you know, and you can change what is being asked of the persons being called.

■ If the response mechanisms being offered are inappropriate, you can change them.

■ If your campaign is flawed, you can pull it!

■ Telemarketing is an effective way to personalize your organization. It allows interaction and an immediate response to questions that might otherwise have "lost the sale."

■ It is likely to have more actual reach than direct mail and mass media because the message begins when the telephone is answered.

■ Calls can be made at times when more people can be found at home, thereby achieving higher response rates.

■ The response rate for telemarketing calls is usually much higher than for mass media or direct mail alone. Anecdotally, telemarketing achieves ten times the result of leaflets or mass media. If coupled with a follow-up letter, this result can often rise to about 25 times higher than leaflets or mass media.

Disadvantages

■ There is often a high acquisition cost per donation for purchased prospect lists.

■ Once a novel way of selling, telemarketing has now become a nuisance to many people. Most dislike receiving telemarketing calls during mealtimes!

Continues on next page

Telemarketing may not always achieve the goal of sustained acquisition of supporters. Often people will give once just to get rid of the caller.

EMAIL AND TEXT MESSAGES

Organizations that appeal to young adults, in particular, should consider the advantages and disadvantages of email or text messages delivered to mobile/cell phones. (Note: Because this is a relatively new method used by only a few organizations at present, insufficient research has been done on its success or failure.)

Advantages

- This method can be a very effective way to reach younger target audiences.

- It can be very highly targeted to different market segments, and response success (or otherwise) will be known almost immediately.

- It supports the notion of urgency of your cause and thereby justifies why you are asking for financial support.

- This method can be relatively inexpensive if your organization has the technological expertise to use it. (If not, the set-up costs may make it prohibitive.)

Disadvantages

- SPAM filtering on emails may mean your message is never read.

- There may be laws against sending emails to people who have not requested them.

- If those in the target audience do not regard your message (especially text) as relevant to them, they are likely to react negatively to your cause and relay this negativity to others.

- If supporters are generated from this method, they may expect all communication in the future to arrive in this form. Can you sustain that kind of program?

- It is likely to generate spontaneous support that can disappear to another cause just as rapidly.

Evaluating Methods and Timing

Whatever method you choose, a financial outlay will need to be made. However, this should be seen as an investment, with an expectation of a return on funds invested, rather than as an expense.

It is important that you don't just pick the cheapest method. Often this will be the choice of those within your organization who control the finances. Rarely is the cheapest method a good long-term investment. Instead, use the method that is best for your organization. Remember, the key goal in donor acquisition, as opposed to just acquiring donations, is to generate long-term supporters for your organization. Long-term supporters bring in ongoing financial support for little additional financial outlay.

Which method should you choose? Look at:

■ How much money you have to spend and the value each method will give you for those funds.

■ Your brand recognition, or lack of it, when choosing which method to use. It will affect your response rates.

■ The advantages and disadvantages of each method as applied to the particular needs of your organization. Do not compare each method with what has worked for other organizations or what is currently in vogue.

■ Good mechanisms for carefully recording your responses. It will be difficult to measure the outcome of the method you use if you fail to capture the information adequately in the first place.

■ Benchmarking with other organizations like yours to see what they have done and what results they have achieved.

After deciding which method works best for your organization, ensure that the timing of the campaign is considered. You don't want to conflict with other campaigns or events, which your organization or others might be holding, that would make your campaign less effective or even inappropriate.

Ensure your campaign, including the material and method chosen, has been cleared (if necessary) with others in your organization. Duplication of effort within a fundraising department or conflict with other departments does no one any good and can cause ill will within an organization.

BEFORE you begin the process of acquiring donors, you need to ensure what will happen AFTER your donor-acquisition campaign is fully developed. It is useless to obtain new donors if you have no plans for how to keep them, and you need to include those plans in your campaign materials.

Your plans need to consider the following.

- When you receive inquiries from potential donors, who will handle them? Do you have more information prepared to provide to them if they seek it? If they question facts stated by your organization in your request for support, can you respond appropriately?

- When you receive a donation, how will it be handled? Can you respond quickly with a thank-you letter, text or email? What other information will you send with the thank-you letter? Have you thought about writing a donor's "bill of rights," telling donors what they can expect from being involved with your organization? (These rights might include being treated with respect, that donations are used for the purpose intended, that donor preferences regarding how often they are solicited are honored, that their right to privacy is of paramount importance.)

- What is the next step? Keep in mind that the purpose of donor acquisition is to acquire long-term donors. Have you considered producing newsletters to keep them informed?

- What records will you keep to remember donor information, their personal preferences and the donations they have made? Are these records required for legal reasons in addition to being good accounting and donor-management practice?

- How will the data you keep be used? Do you have legal issues to consider? What are they and how will they be handled?

Knowing the answers to these questions is crucial to your acquisition plans. The method you choose will need to reflect the answers as will the materials you prepare for the campaign.

REVIEWER'S COMMENT
It bears repeating that you should not embark on a donor-acquisition program unless you have a solid retention plan. Don't do it!

THE CREATIVE BRIEF

Once ongoing-donor strategies are in place, then, and only then, is it time to get started on your acquisition program design.

Start by putting together a document called a creative brief. This will help you identify and articulate all the key issues you need to address, and help you share that information within your organization and with external suppliers.

You need to address the following issues in your creative brief.

- Background. This is an overview of your organization and the services or products it delivers to address your cause.

- Description of your donor program. This is a clear description of all the features and benefits of becoming a donor and the needs that being a donor satisfies for your organization. Your work in designing a continuing-donor program will help you write this section of the creative brief.

- Objectives of communication. You need to be specific here. What do you want to achieve in both the number of donors and the quality of your relationship with donors?

- Marketplace. What's happening with other organizations or causes? Are they conducting donor-acquisition campaigns? If so, what are they doing and how will it affect your plans?

- Description of target audience(s). Who do you want to address and is there more than one group? Provide as much detail as possible on the following (where applicable).
  - ❑ Geographic region
  - ❑ Demographics (male, female, age group, education level)
  - ❑ Giving behaviour of donors: When do they give? Why do they give – what motivates them to give, what benefit do they derive from giving?
  - ❑ Are they unaware, aware, interested, or excited about what your organization does?
  - ❑ Is there loyalty or potential loyalty to your particular organization, or are the donors primarily interested in the cause you champion?

- What do the target audience(s) currently think and feel about your organization?

Continues on next page

- What do you want your target audiences to think and feel? This is where you might consider the motivational triggers.

- Unique Selling Position (USP): What is the single most important thing you want the various target audiences to take from this communication?

- What personality and tone are required in the finished creative piece that is produced? Make sure this fits with the values of your organization.

- Are there any other issues that may assist the creative process? What else should be considered? If you have negative issues, this is the time to note them down.

- What campaign method did you decide to use – leaflets, mass media, direct mail, telemarketing, email and text messaging, or a combination?

- What action(s) do you want? What do you want the target audience to do as a result of receiving this communication?

- Are there any specific incentives you can offer to motivate those in the target audience to take action and become donors? Are there any legal implications involved in offering incentives? For example, if you promise a free music CD to all new donors, would this be counterproductive or have legal implications? Often a better incentive is to speak about lives changed or medical research accomplished due to charitable gifts. This is where the power of good storytelling can have an impact.

- What are the organization's logo, print styles and colours, registration number (if appropriate), telephone numbers, facsimile numbers, email address, website address, and other organizational requirements that you must use?

- What deadlines have you set?

- What budget have you set?

THE CREATIVE BRIEF

▪ What further strategies have you considered? Are you going to follow up this first communication with another?

If you are working with a group of suppliers such as graphic artists, copywriters, printers, mail-distribution companies, list suppliers, or telemarketing-service suppliers, why not invite them all to one or more planning sessions where you provide them with the creative brief? You will all learn a great deal from one another and together build a very strong sense of purpose as well as a strong desire to succeed.

As suppliers realize that they are part of an important logistics chain, their joint creativity might well work to your advantage. None will want to be part of something that isn't going to work. Suppliers will speak out and make suggestions on how your campaign can be improved. There is great

incentive for suppliers to cooperate because they can potentially gain new business from others in the group by demonstrating expertise in their fields.

One final idea needs to be shared about getting started.

You should ALWAYS incorporate some testing to ensure that when you have a creative piece ready, it truly appeals to your target audience and evokes a positive response. Don't fall into the trap of showing it to people inside your organization. They are not objective enough and THEY ARE NOT THE TARGET AUDIENCE!

Instead, why not go back to the leaders who gave you advice about whom to target? Let them see your creative brief. Take note of their feedback. It might be a great use of your time, and it will help them feel that you value their judgment and opinions.

Don't expect miracles or base your goals on what you must achieve to get the financial results you want. Investigate the likely range of response rates you might expect to achieve using the methodology you have chosen.

Set your goals on the lower end of that range. Anything higher than this that you achieve will then be a resounding success!

Likewise, you should set evaluation criteria. How will you know that your donor-acquisition program is successful? How will others know? Who will monitor response rates? What action should be implemented if the response rates underperform? Is your expected average donation being achieved? If not, what can you do to lift it?

Above all else, before you begin, make sure you give yourself a pat on the back for having the will to try to gain new donors for your organization!

Once you've done your planning and your campaign has begun, sit back, enjoy the experience, learn from your mistakes, and think about what you will do differently next time.

REVIEWER'S COMMENT
You may need to build an understanding within your organization of the need to have a donor-acquisition program. It is often the first strategy to go because of the costs and perceived poor returns. This is usually because people don't understand the goals of such a program. Remember, acquiring new donors offsets natural attrition and is vitally important to maintaining the long-term viability of your organization.